FOCUS FLOWZ IN SEASON-SHED

TABLE OF CONTENTS

HOPE'S WELL... 3
SPR!NGIN' FORWARD... 4
SUMMERSHINE ALIGNED... 13
FALLIN' BACK... 22
WINTER WONDERZ... 31
SPRINGIN' AGA!N... 40
RENOWN REALITY... 49

DOUBLE-EDGED P!ECE 22z... 50

SPRING3... 51
SUMMER SQU∧RED... 57
FALL FORT!FIED... 63
WINTER'z WON... 69
SPRING 4WORD... 75
WELL WISHES... 77

Hope's WELL

From less is more, while tests
push & Pull us to discover the
source of it all.
Where it's rough right now becomes a
cause of called trust in rising—from any misstep
or minor fall.

SPR!NGIN' FORWARD

After retraction comes renewed tests, trials, & better paths of invested passion.

INITIAL FIGHT

Outta sight, out of line,
while **designs of mind
help find worth tied
to initial fights**.

Right now, long lasting
lights place more tamed
esteem into dedication;
a stronger, but more
rigorous plight.
**Even enlightened by this
unique brightness**, swinging through
life, there is nothing
more frightening-or-fulfilling
than crowned initial flight.

**Permanent purpose was
granted by guided rights**;
the ones that carryover &
bridge to new life.

This is Habitual fight & flight.

STONE & GEMS

Dust is a conclusion
of time left to illusions,
which fuel proven
changes of substance.

Arranged pieces buffer
previous mindframes, &
gems **brighten the luster of
freshly adjusted aims.**
Truly taming dusk to
dawn, I fill the day
with trusted treasure,
while wild weather flushes
aims of false Judgment away.

**Everything touched then enhanced
brings about more substance,**
never rushing routes to
better views; even after seen
demands of keen adjustment.

ROOTS 2 BLOOMS

A state of recuperation
related with truth
trapped in routes.
Both at soil's destination,
recreated destiny made blooms
a heavily vetted cue.

Today is **a banner
for the ranks** of
tanked motive; as
some motion can't be
grown with, supernaturally going
against the groove of
embedded roots.

Once found, it suits a
different view; **one tied
to evolution, and improved
solutions too.**

PARADIGM

**There are set times,
& their shifters-**
while mixtures of give &
take relate to the
ways of today, then
create way more vigor.

With history tied to
current tendencies, **givers tend
to attract more** enemies
of harmony than heirs.
In mess, prevalent scenes
become less alarming when
time aligns to designed
lack of care.

As mind shifts,
it provides a gift
to givers; **in ways, wins
& winds of wise air.**

Okay, we know what's
found in present times-
so now is also
full of the essence
to shift them.

CARPE DIEM

I see **the day is meant
to be seized**, remaining
pleased with amazing scenes
of strength.

In efforts to receive
relief, scenes becomes sweeter
as weaved ways become
**a stamp of belief
in** their links.

7 in a week,
all leading to increased
peaks of thinking, daily
plans & being.
**Carpe Diem-
the breakthrough's brink.**

GEARS

As gears switch,
tough years instill a
hitch, but which one
fits this?
Is it the one
finding it better
to quit, viewing sticky
situations & seeing them
as too risky?
Or is it stored for
**the roar of the
limitless?**

Inbound Instance, as another
hitch **following take-off
says** the hovering worldly
limits never existed.

Bear witness to missions
in rare frontiers- inching up
through righteous fear, to
truly **stick around for
daring gear switches**.

AERIAL RELAY

Residing where dreams rarely
earn flight, tuned signs
forever fly;
perpetually why **my eyes
are filled with a
hunger for learning still**.

While fighting sights of
concern, new jumpstarts earn
more than just material
feel.
Even still, this shielded light
of life sprouts from
a built temple inside-
despite time always yearning
ahead of pivotal hills.

In healing- yield's movement
is rejuvenated sight **of
real keys, which ignite
timed heights**; helping fully
see past all false
earnings, & cheap thrills.

DREAM'S FOCUS

In bubbles of sense
& serenity, the blooms
tied to memory **removed
all misguided energy**.
Letting fortune find it,
mindless mention bended into
vision seen under time's
design; **then approached higher
assignment** in gear.

Sensing grind's intent can't
mix with lackluster footprints,
limits will appear in all
yields to be convinced
or blinded by fear;
until the bubble pops
& dreams mix **with
an infinite flow** of
newly focused tiers.

SUMMERSH!NE ALIGNED

Past rays don't compare with today's way,
because it gleams most by renewed faith.

Captivated Compass

Areas undiscovered force tangible
rubber to burn out,
leaning toward a conviction
seated in exploring hoarded
order; because it never
overflows any testing border.

Adored words & **wisdom attained**
gave a sore stain to
new charters; while newly
known ignorance quickly
departed then,
from false mental fortune.

Poise & grown work in
water ranges will bend to
let soothing currents in;
knowing now what was
meant as noise, forever
**turns into a trustee
hymn** sowed with new
motion's portion.

Bounty on the Boundless

Facing or relating to
no bounds but
the one who found me
in lost rounds.
No longer limited by
what was around, grounds
of contained manner stood
until one true bound
sounded off; and so
released was all hindrance.

Retrieving what was initially
sent for well being
means being more diligent
than ever, **still protecting
steady intention**.

Being of faith is
one infinite season-
beam, **especially seeing
the worldly will** always
try hardest to keep
boundless kin restricted.

Direction

Full throttle with full bottles
en route to the top.
It's shots in memory of
the ones life forgot, and
more popping for those who
never knew **what was
in their graceful plot**;
being stopped in torn
Trots of courage.

When directed, troubled steers
pass; never subtracting
clear vision of course.

I was rowing, but
crashed ashore onto
perfect timing's island;
once assured we just
**form the less given,
to feel more.**

Striver's Strid3

This faucet of faith
will always keep fueled
state in play.
Unmistaken, effective pace is
unshaken by scene delays;
especially peering so many
lose, moving too
soon in brewed days.

Knowing gems of
growth must first parade
through self-belief, it
revives a divine purpose;
only **fully sound & serene
when renewed to the T.**

Aligned by Design

Breaths automatically became
bridges, which then
fixed what broke
& became left in old
ranges.
As more pieces are
steadily swept & played,
the puzzle begins to **respect
a revitalized sway**;
health woven to
horizon's bold claim.

**When unbending bridges are
created**, make way for
new waves of arrangement.

Tames of design won't
ever let those be
barriers to grown
grace, so **they hone
rarity applied in cadence**;
forever tied to patient aims.

Tested Treasure

Pieces turned into **Peace
revolving**, & released all ties
to weak causes.
Watch wrapped up losses soften;
then turn Into a race
against timed deceit.

Knowing no defeat **with
deep roots overstood**,
the hands leveled with
supreme truth-
gracing a constant loop
of improvement.

Sometimes gruesome, sometimes
glorious; **forever being
a limitless source of reach**.

Leader Utop!a

Grounds rumble with the
stride of humble giants.
Never Boastful, but the
steps made in silence
can't be mistaken for
violent; only relaying more
light when heightened.

Divinely boisterous, but never
unruly, looking around,
rightfully observing sound tuning
of abundance aligned.

No need for stomping,
when the coming grace
brings energy too major
for any mimics, and
too rich for most
to humbly invite.
Seeing this, the best
way **to trump headaches
of ground searches**,
is found sight in
purpose ignited.

LAUNCHERZ ALIGNED

Soak in the beginning,
shoot for the
end goal; but only
if it's envisioned winning.
Golden traces either bring
ending to limits,
or move inches closer
to intended wisdom-

But with them steady
spinning & striking, spinning & striking,
intuition connects light with
missing links in a related
maze.

Forgiving the broken starts,
keep focus on freedom
in another trend of
pace; with unbreakable heart.
A question worth asking
today is, the cause
of begins- which tend
to make bigger ripples
in test filled tenses &
lightning's space.

FALLIN' BACK
[AUTUMN-OMY]

Most times, the first step in
sprouting is back by sound realization.

Forces

**Energy moves smoothly through
mind, while certain** wrinkles
of time conduct their
own vices of worth.

Guides are gems unforced,
but costly pressures of
misfortune played a
role in corroded self-trust.
When dispersed, so is
an unfortunate resort
of lost inner touch.

Fortunately the push/pull
of our universe is
seamed even to rusty
domains, still thrusting forward
while **entrusted to untuck &
rearrange forces**.

Blurred

At first, second
& third thoughts cleared
unresolved hurt.
Then I observed turf
to be covered & found
its map impossible to
put before true recovery.

At the sum of discovery,
it's felt when spirit
buffers; poking &
prodding the drum of
a tenacious journey, which
could always be rougher.

**Finally covering tunes away
from a clustered scene**,
seams only uncover trust
in clarity's hover,
through all urgent scenes;
which are never fatal
as seemed.

Lion's Heart/Eagle View

Relay played part in
negated heals, thinking dissolved
feelings actually dealt with
limited ways.
In this, **a vacant race
erased tasteless blueprints**
never meant for misplacement;
& in the hands of hatred,
all plans exclude known
relation or cause.

One man can lead a
nation, **but healing
will forever come** from
cleared fear; collective
traces of sheer grace &
faith.

Diligence N' Motion

Within the grasp of
grace,
Seeing everyday as a
race to the more
refined mold in physical
places.
As **tied laces hug the
feet of a roamer**,
forever adjust pace & patience.

Active learning in place
of any unleveled setting,
Forever play witness to every
diamond's special illumination.

Clear or in disarray,
faith says it could be
today, or way beyond
the say of a
gem under pressure daily.
A wise man once said
nothing, in order to
hear what devotion declared.
It said stay prepared;
shaking the wait's weight.

Climb

Glitches only prevail when
vision is limited.
Wrestling today's best, shine
on current trails bring
newly lit investment; into
**presence of mind &
winning instance**.

Being too farsighted frightens
long distance grind- **while
alignment comes with gifted
time**; as signs come
with true reflection tied
into vibrant hitches.

Humbly fitting, is a
cause-filled climb, so
do like the times;
fully appreciate every minute.

Yin-Yang

As the leaves, Fall lays
between two extremes of
being.
One second is relief
from roars of raging
heat, and **next is**
belief of any harnessed
rays from last season
to carry through
Winter breeding.
Polar opposites, but they frame
the same meaning; **meeting**
another seam of spring-
a cascading ring.

In bold times, a
lunge assumes after retreat.
As shown in global
heartbeats, after depletion most
times is value, valiantly
seen through life's line;
habitual fall springs.

Conquerors

Calculated risk for **real reward**,
but trained action supports
gradual motion forward.
Foregoing the stance in
demand by worldly plan,
any damage is nothing
more than demise's aim.
However, Wielding anointed hands,
strong ones withstand any
opposing plan's fortune or stain.

Joined forces with warriors
who view lightwork as
urgent, surely creates a
temple of collective steppers.
Once the reps are respected,
just weather will always
plant & grant more gain.

Conquerors withstand the mug
of marsh bends,
then fight to march through;
**only to never bend
again**.

ELEVATED VIEW

Before it gets old, we're
supposed to ensure its
resolved. **As serenity calls
an early pause-**
it sees mixed feelings
find crafty ways to
evolve; & take root.

Without limits, **unguided
grit grows**, so proclaimed
love is made to
push dissolved view.

With initial cause,
Pivotal tosses of truth
awaken **& find ways to
cross out tasteless aims**.
Once replaced with
new ranges to uncover,
it suits a renewal;
to elated view.

WINTER WONDERZ

Even In Wonder, the maze is won.

Wonder'z Weapon

The gray areas of life reside
to provide new grace.
& in the prism
of lost paces,
new faith comes into
play; laying out viewed
days and prayers of
wisdom.

Distorted to Determined

As serenity flowed,
focus trailed the lead
of light; and in hindsight,
all fights were worth the
peace currently transmitted.

Trained **damage couldn't
stand demands of revealed
vantage**, but instead
became fully diminished
by implanted essence;
still advancing with intention.

Now is a panoramic
plan with consistent stance,
guiding renewable chance &
insisted foolproof attention.

This is serene **strength at
a glance** giving missions
to shaved minutes.

3RD Eye Blueprint

Drawn designs grind out
mind's motion, to grow
budded alignment.
Shining more by the
side of dawns raise
confined question,
always followed by free
flowing response.

Humming emotion invoked
a thundering rift of
sums, which then split
to **light molded maps**.
For healthy attention,
the shifts constantly hunger.

A clear lens says,
quickly revealed is true
intent; **even in a
timeless speck's track**.

Wonder close 2 War

Sometimes wonder is wasted,
showing real wounds are
still here; waiting to
be healed.
In springs or basked summer
days, ways never yield
until good use is
made of truth's shield.

Winner's thought when facing
chilling winds, regardless of
past tense, is **shifted
triumph** from beginning to
end.
It's never if, just
when cold will be
overcome-with the fire of
belief in humble heels.

Trust freezes still in
the frame of what's
done, **as coming chills
reveal wins of lasting
battle's tilt.**

Frozen Trackz

Unshaken by acts of
chaos, because they froze
& ceased on the
day I sowed into
broken tracks.
Although hopeless, I can't
deny the motion even then,
was **ever-focused**;
but brewed with the
wrong scope.

SInce noticing, those tracks
have frozen in time;
just as known traits
escape mind once aligned
with higher fate's hope.

For those who relate
in a golden pace's tote.

In Reach, Ins!ght

**On the brink of
new**, old tests try
making true views dilute.
so as black & white
lies lose a deceiving grip
on who was, breakthroughs
continue bringing fueled sources
of use.

The world pushes good
to its furthest corners,
only to prove lack
is most tasteful surrounded
by wasteful hunger;
with both sights respected
& humbly reachable by you.

The ones worth fighting
for are always visions
stamped in daily grooves,
poking at blooms before
**slowly finding now's cue
in eventual tunes**.

Bundled Abundance

A bunch of drowned functions
stumbled into another,
uncovering a quest's rumbling
desire.
Grounded Intention strips
rubber, which burned trying
to smother **newly
inspired pavement.**
It didn't take long
to see higher is
discovered through ladders of
pace & patience.

What's caused will come,
so trust rumbles as
an agent of confirmation.
Bundled abundance, is a
weight only **fit for ones
who understand hidden
balance;** &
the wonder of waiting.

Rise-Rose

First Sight of a
height unknown by any
who won't seek grown
good.
A rose knows at
first sow that its pedals
will grow & pursue
truth from old roots,
although some thorns reveal
stems of outgrown suits.

Phases embolden true current's
throne; flowing consistently as
told by the sun.
Rays in new ones
roll like **risen pedals**
of each level, caressing
a light that shines
on the same settled
soil of proof.

SPRINGIN' AGA!N

From the worst conditions came better intent, & a newly sensed course of vision.

Vivid Vitality

Encounter enough dirt and
it grants a new burst
of recognition;
**one move that must
be made first**,
a final decision of worth.

Is entrusted view only a
limit in troubled turf?
Is this newfound turf
final position,
or another condition of
undying spark-searching
missions?

In hindsight it's seen
how light partners with
vitals to polish dirty
emblems; tuning work
in service **to bridge
with space of clear,
sound, wisdom.**

DAILY BREAD'z RELATED VIEW

Tamed ways of **heart
gave a graceful start**
to patient sparks.
In case of due
opposition, they're encased by
boundless faith.
This tethered space bombarded
every tasteless domain with flavor,
embedded into reality's race.

A savory taste of
**favor gave more face
value** within the ring
of calling's pull; in
the same way, lightened
heart sparked patience.

Seeing change is forever
tamed by its agent,
I stay with the force
who moves the won pace.
Under highest rule, stationed
grind grants daily bread
for infinite jewels & relay.

GOOD IS GOLD

A path stationed to
be trodden by few,
turned into multiple views
of the same embodied
route.

When dirt turns into
worthy road,
you suddenly know;
wherever traction leads, is
loaded with working truths.

Renewed versions of old
view, armed purely into
rolling roles- keep learning cued.

Ahead sits decisional
bloom, which is only
golden if chosen
at the foot of
hope's sole fabric.
The most high's goal
    is the gold;
    abiding by
     majesty,
      never
  makeshift rule.

PAST TENSE

Destructive paths left to
their own peril, &
false intent left to
useless tension.
Where has it gone, but
to past tense?
As the clock ticks
renew, as do I.

**Old tricks can't out
last a true eye**,
which provides a rolling
scene with new sense.
Tension passed as did
past tense, **getting past
unruly ways to fly**
with it falling away
from vision's high lens.

DIVINE SILHOUETTES

Hidden sight from **the masses
turned** into daily communion,
which since,
has never left or
faded from life's attraction.
In drastic lines, action
saved all that became
lasting fuel.

Reassured, how divine
light kept fine tuned
shadows at bay.
Jewels swiftly played to
established ways of
living; **while still building
to** break newfound ceilings.

Parameters of one healing,
humble & holy design.

FIGHT & FLIGHT

Balance is believing in
the wind beneath wings,
while achieving within
groundwork of today's being.

Profound as it may seem,
daily rings of true
calling simply seam
with all-in attitude.

**In actual frames of
mind**, the altitude became
centered around whole tokens.
Held & honed, this emboldened
a home tied to
habitual fight for flight-
Until gratitude propelled
to align strides with
seeking light's ring.

AGAINst INfected GRAIN

Sprouting is furthest
from easy when soils
are more depleted
than ever-
but in due lanes,
**better heart struck
& stuck** through sheds.

Instantly arranged by visual
lines; mental mines blow
to fully see grain
get refined, then shine
through all weather sets.

UNION'S FOXUSED ORDER

Built Increments of belief
linked a wish for
peace, to innate longing
for key position.
Unaverted, worth is just;
working under all love
from above.

Notice the highest humbly
gives trust **as intended
dominion to us**, which is the
sole distinction we have
from bears, birds or
even bugs.

In sight of this
grace; **take the day
with relentless faith in
given love**, forever
sending it back on track
to high above.

REALITY
RENOWN

Seeing roots of nourishment,
natural jewels encouraged the renewal;
tracking back to find &
refine tuned jewels of past grooves.

Double-Edged P!ECE 22z

From the old grooms to new
sprouts that rise;
PEACE
Love
&
L!ght

SPR!NG3

Secondary Fight

Designs of mind
help find worth tied
to initial fight.
Even enlightened by this
unique brightness, Permanent
purpose was granted
by guided rights;

The habitual fight.

Gemz Stone

Brighten the luster of
freshly adjusted aims.

With trusted treasure,
everything touched then enhanced
brings about more substance.

Unstained.

Bloomed From The Root

Recreated destiny made blooms
a banner for the ranks;
one tied to evolution,
and new solutions
too.

Pairadigm

There are set times,
& their shifters.
While givers tend to attract
more in ways, wins
& winds of wisdom—
found in present times.

YEARZ

The roar of the
limitless following take-off
says, stick around for
daring gear switches.

SUMMER SQUARED

Compass Time

Seated in exploring
wisdom attained, turns into
trustee hymns.

Bountiful

No longer limited,
still protecting steady
intention;
especially seeing the
worldly will.

Destination

What was in their
graceful plot;
clear vision of course.
Form the less given
to feel more.

Designated Allure

Respect a revitalized sway.
When unbending bridges are
created, they hone
rarity applied in cadence

Invested Treasure

Peace is revolving with
deep roots overstood;
forever being a limitless
source of reach.

FALL FORT!FIED

Forge

Energy moves smoothly
through mind, while certain
gems are unforced,
entrusted to untuck &
rearrange forces.

2view glue

A vacant race
erased tasteless blueprints,
but its healing will
forever come.

Motion Dealt

Tied laces hug the
feet of a roamer,
Playing witness to hear
what devotion declared.

Limbo

Presence of mind &
winning instance.
while alignment comes
with gifted time, fully
appreciate every minute.

Conquest

Real Reward joined forces with warriors, only to never bend again.

WINTER'z WON

Mind/Matter

As serenity flowed,
damage couldn't
stand demands of revealed
vantage, insisted foolproof
attention;
Strength at a glance.

Sighted Intent

Drawn Designs light molded
maps for healthy attention;
even in a timeless
speck's track.

The Better Battle

Showing real wounds shifted
triumph, as coming chills
reveal wins of a
lasting battle's tilt.

Thawed Trax

Ever-focused;
but brewed with higher
fate's hope in a
golden pace.

Unbeatable Abundance

Stumbled into newly inspired
pavement, fit for ones
who understand hidden
balance; &
the wonder of waiting.

SPRING 4WORD

~NOW~
ALWAYS
PR^Y,
PROSPER,
LEARN & Say
YES 2 higher
EVOLUTION.

FF!SS{T}

Foxus Flowz!n Season-Shed [TRUST]